THE WORLD'S BEST JOKES

(THAT YOU'LL REMEMBER)

JAMES BRIGGS

summersdale

THE WORLD'S BEST JOKES (THAT YOU'LL REMEMBER)

An Hachette UK Company
www.hachette.co.uk

Summersdale Publishers Ltd
Part of Octopus Publishing Group Limited
Carmelite House
50 Victoria Embankment
LONDON
EC4Y 0DZ
UK

www.summersdale.com

Printed and bound in Poland

ISBN: 978-1-78783-570-2

Substantial discounts on bulk quantities of Summersdale books are available to corporations, professional associations and other organizations. For details contact general enquiries: telephone: +44 (0) 1243 771107 or email: enquiries@summersdale.com.

CONTENTS

INTRODUCTION

Welcome to *The World's Best Jokes (That You'll Remember)*. It's not always easy memorizing your favourite gags, wisecracks, puns and rib-ticklers, so we've gathered them all in one cheery place for you! From zinging one-liners to tall tales and funny stories with killer punchlines, these are the jokes you'll want to tell your friends and family again and again!

This book finds the funny in the world around us: from the wonders of nature to scrumptious food, scary monsters, sucky school, sports and the brilliant and bad of modern technology. There'll be a few classics along the way, too, so expect the odd visit to the doctor and some knock-knocking at the door. Who's there? Why it's you, armed with a glut of jokes to have your friends and family in stitches. So, sit back, relax and get ready to ride the ROFLcopter!

CHAPTER ONE

AMUSING ANIMALS

Get ready to be tickled by tentacles, made to giggle by gorillas and to do some LOLing at lions. It's time to set the animals free!

A lion decided a joke competition should be held for all animals. The rules were simple: tell your joke to the tortoise, and if it laughs you go free, but if it doesn't laugh, you get eaten. The zebra went first. It told its joke and everyone laughed, except the tortoise. The zebra was munched down. A chimp went next, but suffered the same fate. Everyone was scared, until a moose was pushed forward. Its joke was awful, but the tortoise burst out laughing. Everyone was baffled. The lion asked why the moose's joke was so funny. The tortoise replied, "I just got the zebra's joke!"

What do you call a dog
that can do magic?
A labracadabrador.

Why can't dogs dance?
Because they have two left feet.

I've just started going
out with a tortoise.
We're taking it slow.

I went into a pet shop and asked if
I could buy a goldfish. The shopkeeper
asked if I wanted an aquarium.
I said I didn't care what star sign it was.

**Did you hear about the big punch-up
between the terrapins and the tortoises?
It was turtle carnage.**

When the animals were finally able to leave the ark, Noah told them to go forth, spread their wings and multiply! All the animals did as they were told, until after some time Noah came upon two snakes. They were just lying there, basking in the sun. Noah asked them, "Why aren't you multiplying?" The snakes replied, "We can't, we're adders!"

Did you hear about the crocodile
who ate five tourists in Egypt?
She's in denial.

**I used to go out with an elephant.
He promised he'd never forget me.**

What animal do you not want to be
sitting next to in an exam?
A cheetah.

**What do you call a pig with three eyes?
Piiig.**

Knock, knock.
Who's there?
Interrupting cow
Interrupting cow wh—
Moooooooo!

"I ran a bath for my pet monkey,
but he said it was too hot."
"Monkeys can't talk."
"Mine can."
"Oh yeah, what did he say?"
"Hoo-hoo-ha-ha!"

Three dinosaurs found a magic lamp.
They rubbed it and a genie popped out!
"Greetings, dinosaurs! I will grant you
each one wish. What do you desire?"
"Meat," roared the first one, "I want meat!"
"Your wish is my command,"
and a giant steak appeared.
"And what do you wish for?" the
genie asked the second dinosaur.
"I want it to rain meat!"
"Your wish is my command," and meat
rained down from the heavens.
The genie turned to the third dinosaur
and said, "And what is your wish?"
The last dinosaur licked its lips and said,
"I want a MEATIER SHOWER!"

What kind of shoes do frogs wear?
Open-toad shoes.

What do you call a mummified bird?
Toucan-khamun.

My partner told me to stop
acting like a flamingo.
I had to put my foot down.

What did the fish say when it hit the wall?
Dam.

Doctor, doctor, I can't help
thinking I'm a goat.
How long have you felt like this?
Since I was a kid.

**What do you call a chicken
crossing the road?
Poultry in motion.**

On what side do chickens
have the most feathers?
The outside.

I saw someone chatting up a cheetah once.
**I thought they were trying
to pull a fast one.**

**What do you call a crocodile in a vest?
An investi-gator.**

What do you call a tiger with no eyes?
Tger.

**What happens when a frog's
car breaks down?
It gets toad.**

A panda walked into a bar, sat down and ordered a sandwich. He ate, pulled out a gun and shot the waiter dead. As the panda stood up to go, the bartender shouted, "Hey! Where are you going? You just shot my waiter and you didn't pay for the food!" The panda yelled back, "I'm a panda. Look it up!" The bartender opened a dictionary. "Panda: A tree-climbing mammal of Asian origin, characterized by distinct black and white colouring. Eats, shoots and leaves."

Why do you call your dog Blacksmith?
**Because every time it hears a knock
it makes a bolt for the door.**

**A horse walked into a bar.
The bartender said, "Hey."
The horse replied, "Yes, please!"**

What's black and white and really noisy?
A zebra with a drum kit.

Where do fish store their money?
In the riverbank.

**Did you hear about the unfit
bird that ran a marathon?
It was puffin.**

What do you call a bear with no teeth?
A gummy bear.

"Did you hear about the grumpy bear?"
"Grizzly?"
"No, it just didn't like mornings."

**Did you hear about the lizard who
took revenge on baddies?
It was a karma chameleon.**

A man walked past a pet shop and saw a cute little dog in the window. He went inside and asked the shopkeeper, "Does your dog bite?" The shopkeeper replied, "No, sir, my dog doesn't bite." The man smiled and went to pet the dog, but it growled and bit him. "Oww!" cried the man, "I thought you said your dog doesn't bite!" The shopkeeper replied, "That's not my dog."

How many tickles does it take
to make an octopus laugh?
Ten–tickles.

**What do you get if you cross a
sandwich and a catapult?
A butter-fly.**

What did one chameleon say to the other?
New look?

A camel and a horse are in a bar.
One's got the hump.

Which musician is a bumblebee's favourite?
Sting.

How do you hire a horse?
Stand it on some bricks.

**Where does a dog go when it loses
its tail and needs a new one?**
A retail store.

A woman was driving along when a police officer stopped her. The officer looked in the back of the lady's vehicle and said, "Why are these penguins in your truck?" She replied, "Because they're mine." "You need to take them to the zoo," the police officer said. The next day, the officer saw the same woman driving down the road. They pulled her over again and saw the penguins still in the truck, but they were wearing sunglasses this time. "I told you to take these penguins to the zoo!" the officer said. "I did," the lady replied. "And today we're going to the beach."

Knock, knock.
Who's there?
Owls.
Owls who?
Yes, they do.

**Did you hear about the underwater
bar for mythical sea mammals?
It served no real porpoise.**

A friend asked me to round
up their 28 sheep.
I said, "No problem: 30."

**Why did the animals at the zoo get arrested?
They were lion.**

If you ever need to look like you have
a beard, glue a rabbit to your face.
Hey presto, facial hare!

A dog walked into a job centre and said to the startled assistant, "Hello, got any jobs?" The stunned assistant replied, "You're a talking dog!" The dog said, "Yep, got any jobs?" The assistant gathered herself and said, "Hang on, I'll check." She phoned the local circus. "Hey, I've got a talking dog! Could you use it?" "Sure!" said the circus owner, "Send it over!" The assistant went back to the dog, "I've found you a job." "Awesome! Where?" asked the dog. "The circus," replied the assistant. The dog looked puzzled. "The circus? What do they want with a plumber?"

What do you get if you cross an
octopus with a cowboy?
Billy the Squid.

Why do birds fly south in winter?
Because it's a long way to walk.

Doctor, doctor, people keep
telling me I'm a horse.
Don't listen to those nay-sayers.

What did the tiger say to the leopard?
**Do you always have to wear
that spotty jacket?**

Where do little rodents go on holiday?
Hamsterdam.

**What are the best animals at
explaining things to you?
Squirrels. They always give
it to you in a nutshell.**

A team of little animals and a team of big animals decided that they would play a game of football. During the first half of the game, the big animals were using their size and power and winning easily. But at half time, a centipede came on as a substitute and scored so many goals that the little animals actually won the game. When the game was over, a little mouse asked the centipede, "Where were you during the first half?" The centipede replied, "Putting on my boots!"

Did you hear about the monkeys
that shared an Amazon account?
They were Prime-mates.

**Why should you never hang around
with a hippopotamus and a cheetah?
It gets heavy, quickly.**

Did you know a school of piranha can
devour a child in under a minute?
**Anyway, today I lost my
job at the aquarium.**

I was out for a lovely walk in the woods today when this black-and-white animal came up to me and wouldn't leave me alone. First it followed my every move, then it started rubbing itself against my leg, before making funny noises with its snout. **It just wouldn't stop badgering me.**

What type of bird is best at peering through really small holes?
Peeking duck.

CHAPTER TWO

FARCICAL FAMILIES AND RAUCOUS RELATIONSHIPS

Families and our darling other halves, you can't live with them, you can't live without them. So, to celebrate them, and make them slightly more tolerable, here's a bunch of side-splitters directed right back at the ones you love, laugh at and couldn't think of living without!

I used to date a 10-foot wall, but we broke up.
I never got over it.

I usually meet my partner at 12.59 p.m.
It's our one-to-one time.

My father used to tell me, "You
should always fight fire with fire."
**It's probably why he lost his
job as a firefighter.**

Did you hear what Meatloaf said when
he was asked out by a bank robber?
**He would do anything for love,
but he won't do that.**

My new friend walked into my house and pointed at a family picture on the wall.
"Why have they all got really long legs?" my friend asked.
I replied, "That's my extended family."

**I walked out into the garden with a friend and showed her around.
She said, "Why are those two children and that man sat up there?"
I said, "Oh, that's my family tree."**

My partner dumped me yesterday. He said
our relationship felt like too much work.
At least he gave me two weeks' notice.

Two people were sitting in a kayak but were
really cold. So they decided to light a fire.
But when they did, the boat sank, proving
that you can't have your kayak and heat it.

I told my girlfriend she drew
her eyebrows too high.
She looked really surprised.

A woman had twins and decided to give them up for adoption. One went to a family in Egypt and was named Amal. The other went to a family in Spain, who named him Juan. A decade later Juan sent a picture of himself to his birth mother. When she received the picture, she told her husband she wished she had a picture of Amal, too. Her husband replied, "They're twins. Once you've seen Juan, you've seen Amal."

My grandpa died last week because we couldn't figure out what his blood type was. But he was a strong man who never gave up; he kept telling us to be positive right until the last moment.

One night, a boy woke up and saw an apparition of his father who had recently died. He broke down crying, and screamed out, "I'm sorry!" His father responded, "Hi Sorry, I'm Dead!"

Why are relationships like maths?
**You look at your ex and try
to figure out why!**

**My auntie was a great conductor
– she got struck by lightning.**

My mother-in-law fell down a wishing well.
I thought, "Wow, they really do work!"

**I used to go out with a tennis player,
but love meant nothing to them.**

My wife went into labour unexpectedly at home. I called the doctor and said, "Doctor, doctor, my wife's gone into labour. The contractions are coming really quickly, what should I do?" The doctor replied, "Is this her first child?" I said, "No, it's her husband."

"I'm going to the British coast
next week," I said to a friend.
"Seeing Wales?" they asked.
I said, "No, my grandma."

**My family say they're worried about
my addiction to dot-to-dot puzzles.
It's OK, I know where to draw the line.**

I used to be in a relationship with a pirate,
but we didn't see eye to eyepatch.

I saw a man standing outside a cemetery
in the rain. I felt sorry for him so went
over and asked why he was there.
"To see my late wife," he replied.
"Oh, I'm sorry," I said.
**"She's the one that should be sorry; I've
been waiting here half an hour already!"**

**My new boyfriend said he'd got me as
his wallpaper which I thought was really
sweet until he showed me his front room.**

There was a family of balloons: Mummy balloon, Daddy balloon and Baby balloon. Each night, Baby balloon had nightmares and went into its parents' room. Daddy balloon always woke up and said, "Don't worry, it's all part of growing up," and told it to sleep in their bed. But as Baby balloon got older, it couldn't fit any more. One night it released air from Mummy balloon, then from Daddy balloon. But it still couldn't fit, so it released air from itself, too. Daddy balloon woke up, furious at their wrinkled state. He said, "You've let me down, you've let your mother down, but most importantly you've let yourself down."

My partner asked, "Can you make me breakfast in bed?"
I said, "I'm sorry, dear, I'll have to go to the kitchen."

My girlfriend poked me in the eye the other day.
I stopped seeing her for a while.

I got my mother a fridge for Christmas this year.
Can't wait to see her face light up when she opens it.

My partner asked me what I
wanted played at my funeral.
"Football," I said.

**I married a clown once, and we had a
child together. When we got divorced
it turned into a real custardy battle.**

I'm from a failed family of magicians.
I've got two half-sisters.

**Would anyone like to be in a
platonic relationship?
I'm asking for a friend.**

A woman took her seat at the World Cup Final. She looked across and noticed an empty seat between her and the next man. She said, "Who would ever want to miss the World Cup Final?" The man replied, "Oh, it's my wife's seat, we've gone to every World Cup Final together for the last twenty years, but she died recently." The woman said, "I'm so sorry, but what about the rest of your family?" The man replied, "They're at her funeral."

I was late to my cannibal
family's summer BBQ.
They gave me the cold shoulder.

**My parents have asked me to take
over the family trampoline business.
I said I wanted to be a carpenter instead,
but it's something to fall back on.**

A lady was washing the car with her son,
when after a while the son asked, "Do you
think we could use a sponge instead?"

A girl said to her partner, "I can't get these shoes on." Her partner said, "They're on the wrong feet!" The girl replied, "But they're the only feet I've got!"

A penguin went into a bar and walked up to the counter. It asked, "Have you seen my brother?" The bartender replied, "I don't know, what does he look like?"

When I was little, my dad and I went to the zoo to see the birds. I had read about the colourful jungle birds, and even heard that some could talk! I was so excited to hear what they would sound like in person. The first bird we saw was a toucan but I was disappointed to hear that it was just chirping. I turned to my Dad and said, "Dad, can we talk with toucans?" He replied, "Not without a string."

Guess who just woke up to 52 missed calls and 37 messages from their ex?
My ex.

**I've got two kids, five and eight.
We're not very good at naming things.**

My partner said I needed to get some perspective.
I said it depended on how you looked at it.

**I used to be in a relationship with an elevator.
It had its ups and downs.**

Last night my partner and I had a TV marathon. We watched four episodes of a new series back to back.
Luckily, I was facing the TV.

**My grandma has just got a new senior citizen scooter.
It's so fast; it can do
30 aisles per hour!**

A lady who was a hopeless romantic was working away from home. She missed her husband terribly and texted him saying, "If you are laughing, send me your smile. If you are eating, send me a bite. If you are drinking, send me a sip. If you are sleeping, send me your dreams. If you are crying, send me your tears. I love you more than anything in the world!" The husband replied, "I am on the toilet. Please advise what to do…"

I've just started going out with a balloon but it's not really working out. I tried letting her down gently but PFFFFFFFT...

My girlfriend and I have a very complex relationship. I'm real and she's imaginary.

I've been happily married for six years... out of twenty.

My uncle has just started
going out with a boat.
I can't judge; it's their relation-ship.

"Hey Dad, have you seen my sunglasses?"
"No son, have you seen my Dad glasses?"

Met a barcode in the
supermarket the other day.
I got her number.

What do you call a hippy's wife?
Mississippi.

I've been dating some
sandpaper for a while.
It's been pretty rough, actually.

I've been dating a donkey.
It's a bit of an ass.

I just started dating an elephant.
It's already getting a bit heavy.

How do you know when a kid joke
becomes a dad joke?
When it becomes apparent.

One day, when I was younger,
I watched my father cheerily grilling
burgers. When they were ready, he handed
me one and said it was a "bison" burger.
Then he left and never came back.

My friends went mad when they heard I was dating a Shakespeare-loving cockerel.
I think it's much a-cock-a-doodle-do about nothing.

My partner and I share a fantastic sense of humour.
We have to because they don't have one.

What's the difference between an in-law and an outlaw?
Outlaws are wanted.

I used to have an uncle with a rubber toe.
Ah, I miss Uncle Roberto.

CHAPTER THREE

FUNNY FOOD

It's time to feast on some scrum-diddly-umptious food funnies – just be sure not to tell them with your mouth full. Say it, don't spray it!

What do you call a cheese that's not yours?
Nacho cheese.

**What's the best cheese for getting
a bear down from a tree?
Camembert.**

What's the best cheese to hide a horse?
Mascarpone.

**What type of cheese likes to
admire itself in the mirror?
Halloumi!**

I was in a restaurant the other day and I said to the waitress, "How long will my spaghetti be?"
She said, "I don't know, we never measure it."

My sister bet me I couldn't make a car out of spaghetti.
You should have seen her face when I drove pasta.

What did Batman's family say when
he strolled in for dinner an hour late?
Ah, Batman returns.

**Did you hear about the woman who
drowned in a bowl of muesli?
She was pulled in by a strong currant.**

How do you get a hipster to
eat corned beef?
Put it in a man bun.

A girl asked her mother, "Are bugs good for you to eat?" Her mother recoiled and said, "That's horrible! Don't talk about things like that when it's dinner time." After finishing up her dinner the lady turned to her daughter and asked, "Now, what was it you wanted to ask me earlier?" "Oh, nothing," the girl replied. "There was a fly in your soup, but you've already eaten it."

Knock, knock.
Who's there?
Lettuce.
Lettuce who?
Lettuce in – it's freezing!

Doctor, doctor, I think I've got a bit of lettuce sticking out of my bottom.
Looks like the tip of the iceberg to me.

Did you hear about the group
of charming berries?
They were real smoothies.

What do you call a fake noodle?
An impasta.

How did Bob Marley like his doughnuts?
With jammin!

I chatted up a pig the other day.
Pulled pork.

Luke Skywalker and Obi-Wan Kenobi decided to go out for dinner.

"What do you fancy, Luke?" said Obi-Wan.

"I'm not sure. You decide!" Luke replied.

"OK," said Obi-Wan, "let's go for Chinese!"

So Obi-Wan and Luke went into the restaurant and ordered a delicious banquet of food. They tucked in, but Luke found it to be an absolute nightmare. Every time he tried to grab something with his chopsticks it fell onto the table. Obi-Wan looked up calmly and said, "Use the fork, Luke."

I just won the race where you sit on
food for the second year running.
I'm on a roll.

**What does a grape do when it
gets trodden on?
It lets out a little wine.**

What do you call a toasted cheese
sandwich that gets right up in your face?
Too close for comfort food.

"I went for some Indian food at the weekend," I said to my friend.
"Daal?" they replied.
I said, "Not in the slightest, it was bursting with flavour!"

Waiter, waiter!
There's a small slug in my salad.
So sorry, would you like me to exchange it for a bigger one?

An elderly couple went to a fast-food restaurant. They ordered one burger and fries and split it in two. A stranger on the next table said politely, "If you want, I can buy some extra food for you." "No thanks, we've been married fifty years, we share everything," said the couple. Time went by and the stranger could see that only the man was eating. The kind stranger said again, "I really don't mind buying you something." The old man replied, "Don't worry, we share everything." So the stranger asked the woman, "Why are you not eating?" The woman replied, "I'm waiting for the teeth."

I cooked Pancakes this morning.
I thought it was delicious!
My kids didn't; it was their rabbit.

**Where did the spaghetti and
sauce go to dance?
The meat-ball.**

Did you hear about the two French cheese
trucks that smashed into each other?
De brie was all over the road.

Have you ever tried to eat a clock?
So time-consuming!

Why do some people eat snails?
They're not into fast food.

What's the worst meal for a balanced diet?
A see-saw salad.

Did you hear about the man who ate
yeast and shoe polish for breakfast?
Every morning he would rise and shine!

A man was telling his friend about taking his partner out for a delicious dinner to celebrate their special anniversary. He said, "It's absolutely amazing, they make everything right in front of you, there and then!"
The friend, all excited, said, "Oh, wow, I've heard of fancy places like that, it sounds like a real treat. May I ask the name of the restaurant?"
The man replied, "Sure: Subway."

Did you hear about the
restaurant on the moon?
Great food, horrible atmosphere.

Why did the baker stop making doughnuts?
He was fed up of the hole business.

Two plates were dining in the restaurant,
one said to the other, "Lunch is on me."

Knock, knock!
Who's there?
Figs.
Figs who?
Figs the doorbell – it's broken!

I took my partner to a really fancy restaurant last night but after we'd eaten, she kept insisting she pay for the meal. I said, "Don't be stupid, we're halfway down the road. Just keep running!"

A couple driving saw signs for the nearby town of Kissimmee and wondered whether it was pronounced KISSimmee, kissIMMee or kissimmEE. The debate got heated so they decided they would ask a local. They pulled into a fast-food restaurant and stepped up to the counter. The man said, "I know this may sound like a silly question, but could you please tell us very slowly where we are?" The server looked at him and very slowly said, "Buuurrrrgerrrrrrr Kiiiiiiingggggg."

For Halloween we dressed up as cashews.
Everyone said we were nuts.

**What did the cake say to the fork?
Want a piece of me?!**

I burned my Hawaiian pizza the other day.
**I think I needed to cook it at
aloha temperature.**

**If your boyfriend doesn't appreciate
your fruit jokes, let that mango.**

What do you get if you cross a chilli,
a shovel and a greyhound?
A hot-diggity-dog!

**Did you hear about the pilot who
loved to cook while flying?
It was a recipe for disaster.**

A diner looked through all the delicious options on the menu before finally deciding upon their dinner choice. "I will have the octopus," they said. The waiter replied, "Excellent choice! Just to warn you though, it takes five and a half hours to cook." "Five and a half hours? Why on earth does it take so long?" The waiter said, "Well, they keep reaching out and turning the cooker off."

I ate way too much in the holidays.
Now I've gone cold turkey.

Every morning I tell myself I'm going to make pancakes, but then I just keep waffling.

A lot of people cry when they chop onions.
The trick is not to get too close to them.

Did you hear about the guy
who invented Tic Tacs?
He made a mint!

Two peanuts walked into a bar.
One was a salted.

How much room do you need
for fungi to grow?
As mushroom as possible.

Why don't eggs tell each other jokes?
They'd crack each other up.

What do you get when you cross
a cheetah and a hamburger?
Fast food!

**Waiter, waiter! Do you have frogs' legs?
No, they're my own.**

Bread is a lot like the sun.
It rises in the yeast and sets in the waist.

What's orange and sounds like a carrot?
A parrot.

**What do you get when you cross
a dinosaur with a pig?
Jurassic Pork!**

Becoming a vegetarian...
That was a giant missed steak.

**What do you call a little green vegetable
that breaks out of prison?
An esca-pea!**

Did you hear about the boy band Bananas?
They split.

**I ordered a chicken and an egg from Amazon.
I'll let you know.**

CHAPTER FOUR

TITTERING TECHNOLOGY

What's faster than a speeding bullet, smarter than a dictionary and makes your life easier? No, it's not Superman sitting in a library doing your homework – it's technology! So, fire up your computers and tell everyone on social media you've got more technology funnies than a Silicon Valley clown convention!

What did the Bon Jovi satnav say when
the journey was 50 per cent complete?
Woah, we're halfway there!

**What's the best way to get Bluetooth?
Eat a blueberry.**

The internet generation are
so self-absorbed.
It's all meme, meme, meme.

**I beat my brother on the PlayStation today.
I consoled him.**

Did you hear about the kid who boasted about being addicted to his smartphone?
He was appy and he knew it.

A computer walked into a bar. All of its friends had been waiting for ages. They said, "Where have you been, we've been waiting for an hour!" The computer replied, "Sorry, it was a hard drive."

Doctor, doctor. I think I'm
addicted to Twitter.
Sorry, I don't follow you.

What computer sings the best?
A Dell.

What did one device say to the other?
Are you syncing what I'm syncing?

Doctor, doctor, I can't stop copy-and-pasting.
Doctor, doctor, I can't stop copy-and-pasting.
Doctor, doctor, I can't stop copy-and-pasting.
Doctor, doctor, I can't stop copy-and-pasting.
Doctor, doctor, I can't stop copy-and-pasting.
Doctor, doctor, I can't stop copy-and-pasting.
Doctor, doctor, I can't stop copy-and-pasting.
Doctor, doctor, I can't stop copy-and-pasting.
Doctor, doctor, I can't stop copy-and-pasting.
Doctor, doctor, I can't stop copy-and-pasting.

An SEO expert walked into a bar,
bars, pub, tavern, public house, inn,
themed bar, drinks, beer, alcohol.

A woman was browsing the internet at a
funeral when she asked the priest, "Do you
have the Wi-Fi password?" The priest was
horrified and said, "Respect the dead!"
The woman replied, "All lower case?"

My partner asked what's on the television.
"Dust," I said.

I tried to use "beef stew" as my computer password, but it wasn't stroganoff.

Where do the cool mice live?
In their mouse pads.

**Why did the computer keep sneezing?
It had a virus.**

A man was at home on a cold winter's evening, and sent his partner a text: "Windows frozen!" His partner, busy at work, quickly thought of a solution and replied, saying, "Use some warm water." A little while later the man's partner received a reply: "The computer is smoking!"

What is an astronaut's favourite
place on a computer?
The space bar.

**Why did the man store his
money in the freezer?
He wanted cold, hard cash.**

The inventor of autocorrect
passed away today.
Restaurant in peace.

I was looking for my record player
when I realized I was sitting on it.
I'd been going around in circles.

**Why did the hobbit set their
smartphone to vibrate?
They were scared the ring
would give them away.**

I was at home relaxing the other day when all of a sudden a burglar burst into my front room. He shouted, "Give me your wallet and nobody gets hurt." I simply laughed in his face and said, "Alexa, get the police." Next thing I knew, I had no wallet and all I could hear was Sting singing "Roxanne".

I love my satnav.
I'd be lost without it.

**How does Dracula find his
way to his victims?
Batnav.**

I bought a satnav from Bono,
but it doesn't work.
I still haven't found what I'm looking for.

I asked my girlfriend how to turn Alexa off.
She said, "Try walking round the house naked."

**The Grim Reaper came for me last night but I fought him off with my brand new vacuum cleaner.
Talk about Dyson with death!**

I hear voices in my head, but only when I wear headphones.

**I got a TV with broken sound for next to nothing.
I couldn't turn it down!**

A woman walked into a coffee
shop and asked the barista
for the Wi-Fi password.
The barista replied, "You need
to buy a drink first."
The woman ordered a coffee, and
a muffin for good measure. She
asked the barista again, "Can you
tell me the Wi-Fi password now?"
The barista said, "You need to buy a
drink first, all lower case, no spaces."

I put my phone in airplane mode the other day, but it just sat there doing nothing.

What do you get if you cross a computer with an elephant? Lots of memory!

Doctor, doctor, I think I've swallowed a Wi-Fi router. **Oh no! How are we supposed to get the Wi-Fi code now?**

"What did our parents do before
the internet?" I asked my sister.
**She didn't know and nor did
my fifteen brothers.**

Did you hear about the monster made out
of wires, smartphones and routers?
He was a tech giant!

An old man was visiting his son and daughter-in-law for the weekend. He was sitting in an armchair when he asked if he could borrow a newspaper. The son snorted with laughter and said, "Dad, this is the twenty-first century!" The daughter-in-law chipped in, "We don't waste money on newspapers. Here, why don't you borrow my iPad instead?" The old man said, "Great, thanks. That fly won't know what's hit it!"

I've decided to sell my vacuum cleaner.
It was only collecting dust.

Last week I got stuck in a blender.
Pour me.

What do you call a nun sitting
on a washing machine?
A sistermatic!

While making my lunch the other day
I put a baguette in the microwave.
It was a French revolution!

Every year I buy a TV with a
different number of pixels.
It's my New Year's resolution.

**My Bluetooth speaker didn't work
so I threw it in a lake.
Now it's syncing.**

A man was sitting at home when he received a text from his neighbour. "Sorry, I'm using your wife, all day and all night when you aren't home. I'm confessing this to you because I feel guilty. I hope you will accept my deepest apologies." The man was so angry he stormed straight round to his neighbour's house and shot him. A few minutes later he received another delayed text. "Stupid autocorrect! Sorry, I meant Wi-Fi – not wife."

What's a pirate's favourite type of CD?
A CD–Arrrrrr!

**The shovel. Now that's a
groundbreaking bit of technology.**

When technology finally figures out how to
illuminate our homes without light bulbs,
I will be delighted.

What network is Luke Skywalker on?
Yodafone.

Machetes are extremely tech-savvy.
They can hack anything!

A man walked into a radio store and said,
"Woah, there are so many stereo-types."

Why don't fish watch satellite TV?
They like streams.

Did you hear about the IT worker who
quit to become a lumberjack?
They just loved login.

What did the spider do on the computer?
Made a website.

What do computers eat for dinner?
Micro chips.

My partner asked me why I was
speaking so softly while in the house. I said
I was afraid Mark Zuckerberg was listening.
She laughed. I laughed. Siri laughed.
Alexa laughed.

**Have you heard about the latest
pirate technology?
They've got the iPatch.**

How do trees get on the internet?
They log on.

What do you call a blind iPhone?
Phone.

My friend did their PhD in
washing machines.
They're a spin doctor now.

What did Google say when it was asked
for a restaurant recommendation?
Search me.

CHAPTER FIVE

RUDE!

There are many things that are
rude – willies, bums, farts, boobs,
boogers and poop – and they're
right here in this chapter. So, turn
the page and let's get gross!

A child came home from school, sat at the dinner table and said to their parents, "Mum, Dad, the teacher asked a question today and I was the only one in the class who knew the answer!" The parents beamed proudly at one another, pleased with their brilliant parenting, and said, "That's wonderful! What was the question?" The child replied, "Who farted?"

RUDE!

I've been having my morning
poop at 6.45 a.m. every single
day for the past ten years.
It's such a shame I wake up at 7.00 a.m.

**I accidentally swallowed a whole
bag of Scrabble tiles last night.
That could spell disaster for my next poop.**

Have you heard about ninja farts?
Silent, but deadly.

I called up my work yesterday and said,
"I can't come in today, I have a wee cough."
The boss said, "You have a wee cough?"
I said, "Great! Thanks boss,
see you next Monday!"

I got a new stick of deodorant the other day. The instructions say remove cap and push up bottom. I can barely walk, but when I fart the room smells wonderful.

An old married couple were sitting down in church one Sunday as they always did. All of a sudden, the woman turned to her dear old husband and said, "Oh my god, I've just let out a really, really long, silent fart. What on earth am I going to do?" The husband turned to her and said, "Well, first you need to replace the battery in your hearing aid."

What's the best time to go to the toilet?
Poo-thirty.

**What ancient magic makes
you poop yourself?
Voodoodoo dolls.**

What did the poop say to the fart?
You blow me away.

I bought a toilet brush yesterday,
but I still think I prefer toilet paper.

RUDE!

I had to go to the hospital last night as
I had a Disney toy stuck up my bum.
**The doctor just took the
Mickey out of me.**

**A wise man once said: go to sleep with an
itchy bum, wake up with a smelly finger.**

A woman walked into a restaurant and sat down at a table. As she bent down to reach into her bag for her phone, she farted both loud and long. Much to her horror she saw that the waiter was standing right behind her. Mortified, she made eye contact with him and shouted, "Stop that!" The waiter replied, "Yes madam, which way did it go?"

What did one piece of toilet
paper say to another?
I'm totally wiped out.

What's invisible and smells like bananas?
Monkey farts.

Why did the toilet paper roll down the hill?
To get to the bottom.

I like toilets for only two reasons:
number one and number two.

What do you call a teacher who
doesn't fart in public?
A private tooter.

**Doctor, doctor, I've got a
strawberry stuck up my bum!
Don't worry, I've got some cream for that.**

A man walked into a hospital
emergency department with four
plastic horses up his butt.
They described his condition as stable.

RUDE!

Why does Piglet always smell dreadful?
Because he's always playing with Pooh.

**What's brown and sticky
and lies on the floor?
A stick.**

What did Spock find in the
Starship Enterprise toilet?
The Captain's Log.

**What did the policeman say to the man
when he caught him peeing outside?
Urine trouble.**

I desperately needed a poop on the train the other day, but having walked up and down every single train carriage, I discovered all of the toilets were out of order. I couldn't believe it, I had to just sit there and hold it for over an hour. Eventually, the person sat opposite looked at me in disgust and said, "Is that a poop in your hand?"

I farted in an elevator once.
It was wrong on so many levels.

I tried to explain to my six-year-old that it's perfectly normal to accidentally poop your pants, but she's still making fun of me.

My family has a genetic predisposition for diarrhoea.
It runs in our jeans.

Last week someone broke into the
police station and stole the toilet.
The cops say they have nothing to go on.

How do computers go to the toilet?
They log out.

Why did the octopus blush?
He saw the ocean's bottom.

What comes out of your nose at 150 mph?
Lambo-greeny!

One time I farted in a room full of hipsters.
**Then they spent two hours
arguing over who heard it first.**

**Did you hear about the man who brought
toilet paper to the birthday bash?
He was a real party pooper.**

An old lady went to the doctor and said, "I have a problem with frequent gas. Fortunately, the farts never smell and are always silent. I've farted at least ten times since I've been here, and I bet you didn't even notice!" The doctor said, "Take these pills and come back next week." The next week the old lady returned. "Doctor," she said, "I don't know what you gave me, but now my silent farts smell absolutely awful!" The doctor said, "Good! That's your sinuses cleared up, now let's work on your hearing."

Knock, knock.
Who's there?
Europe.
Europe who?
No, you're a poo!

**A man wanted to join the wee-wee club.
The owner thought about it for
a second, then said, "Urine!"**

Why was the sand wet?
Because the sea weed!

What do you call a policeman
standing on a dog poop?
Officer on doody.

Why did the baker's hands smell?
He kneaded a poo.

A cannibal threw up after his last meal.
It's true, you really can't keep
a good man down.

What did one fly say to the other?
Is this stool taken?

A man farted in bed next to his wife. She said, "What in the world was that?" He replied, "Touchdown. I'm winning!" She decided to get even, so she let a fart rip, too. He yelled, "What was that?" She replied, "Touchdown, scores are level!" He wanted to get her back, but he tried so hard that he pooped the bed. The wife asked, "What was that?" The man said, "Half-time, switch sides."

Why can't you hear a pterodactyl
going to the toilet?
Because the p is silent.

I bent over to pick a buttercup.
**Why people leave buttocks lying
around baffles me.**

Why did the toilet paper cross the road?
It was on a roll.

Where does a cow fart come from?
The dairy air.

How do cows do cowpats?
With bowel mooooovements.

A bear and a rabbit were both taking a poop in the woods. The bear turned around to the rabbit and said inquisitively, "Do you ever have trouble with poop sticking to your fur?" "No, I don't, actually," said the rabbit. "That's good to know," said the bear, and then he scooped the rabbit up and wiped his bottom with it.

What do you call a T-Rex's fart?
A blast from the past!

**What's a dog's favourite sport?
Rug-pee!**

What do you call an old fart?
A fartifact!

**I just read a fantastic book
called *Poop Is Great*.
The pro-log section was particularly good!**

Why couldn't the toilet paper
cross the road?
It got stuck in a crack.

Why should you never fart in an Apple store?
Because they don't have Windows.

RUDE!

A man finally managed to convince his long-time crush to go on a date with him. He picked her up in his car, but when the woman reached up to her seat belt she let out a loud fart. She said, "I hope we can keep this just between the two of us!" "Well, if you don't mind," said the man as he opened the window, "I'd rather it spread a little!"

Why was the bottom broken?
It had a crack in it.

What's brown and sounds like a bell?
DUNG!

Why are blacksmiths always
being accused of farting?
Because whoever smelt it, dealt it.

What's the difference between
a grubby bus station and a lobster
with breast implants?
**One's a crusty bus station and
one's a busty crustacean!**

**Did you hear about the teenager
who got his teacher pregnant?
Never mind, it's just a juvenile dad joke.**

CHAPTER SIX

SIDE-SPLITTING SPORT

A lot of people dream of being an Olympic champion, the best quarterback in the world, a soccer star or a tennis legend, right before they realize they have spaghetti limbs, butterfingers and zero coordination. Still, they can have the last laugh with these sporting side-splitters!

If pessimism was an Olympic sport,
I doubt I'd win it.

What is a sheep's favourite game?
Baa-dminton!

I just found an origami sports channel.
It's paper view.

A tennis ball walked into a bar.
The bartender asked,
"Have you been served?"

I went to the gym earlier and thought I'd hop on the treadmill. Then people looked at me strangely, so I decided to jog instead.

Knock, knock!
Who's there?
Canoe!
Canoe who?
Canoe come over and play?

Two potatoes were watching a sports match. One turned to the other and said, "You're a real commentator!" The other turned and said, "Who are you calling common?"

How many golfers does it take to change a lightbulb? Fore!

I called the local gym and enquired about their yoga classes. They asked, "How flexible are you?" I said, "I can't do Tuesdays or Thursdays."

A cricket hopped into a sports shop and said to the shopkeeper, "Do you sell baseball bats?" The shopkeeper was shocked to see a talking cricket, but had a lot of crazy customers over the years, so just said, "Yes, there are some over there," before adding: "By the way, did you know there is a sport named after you?" The cricket looked back and said, "Really? You have a sport called Roger?"

Two people were sitting in a football stadium waiting for the game to start. One turned to the other and said, "I hope the rain keeps up." "Why's that?" replied the friend. "So it doesn't come down!"

Doctor, doctor, I've got a cricket ball stuck up my butt.
How's that?!
Oh, don't you start!

Why is camping the new extreme sport everyone's talking about?
It's in tents.

I used to go out with a tennis player
who was a total love machine.
They were rubbish at tennis.

I used to have a book about
boomerangs. I lent it to somebody,
but it never came back.

How did Scrooge end up with a football?
The ghost of Christmas passed.

A man was out hunting when he accidentally shot his partner. He picked up his phone and called the emergency services. "Help!" he screamed into the phone, "I was trying to shoot a deer and accidentally killed my friend." "All right," said the operator, "try to calm down. First, I need you to make sure they're dead." "Hold on a second," replied the hunter. Suddenly, there was a bang, and the hunter came back on the line, "Yeah, he's dead now."

A woman knocked on my door
and asked for a small donation
for the local swimming pool.
**I went inside and brought
her a glass of water.**

**My tennis opponent wasn't very
happy with my serve.
They always returned it.**

A friend of mine had a brush
with the law last night.
**They were playing against
the police curling team.**

Knock, knock.
Who's there?
Uriah.
Uriah who?
Keep Uriah on the ball.

Two waves had a race.
They tide!

A man walked into a stable looking for a racehorse. "I've got just the horse for you," said the owner. "Only thing is when you want it to stop you need to shout, 'Woah there' and when you want it to go you say, 'Thank God'." The man nodded and took the horse for a ride. They raced at breakneck speed across many fields when the man saw a cliff ahead. "Stop!" he shouted. But the horse kept going. No matter what he tried the horse wouldn't stop. Finally, he remembered the words, "Woah there." The horse skidded to a halt just a few inches from the edge of the cliff. The man looked up to the sky and said, "Thank God."

I met a girl who was really into sports. She said she had to look after a goal and stop the ball getting in there, no matter what. **That was when I knew, she was a keeper.**

Did you hear about the canoe shop that announced it was giving away all its canoes for free? It was a real oar deal.

Why did the golfer wear two pairs of trousers? **In case he got a hole in one.**

Why are penguins the best racing drivers?
They're always in pole position!

**I just came back from a co-worker's funeral
who died when he was hit on the head by
a tennis ball. It was a lovely service.**

Why didn't the dog play football?
It was a boxer.

**Did you hear about the sad case
of the bowling bowl?
It ended up in the gutter.**

You are stuck in a closed iron box.
All you have inside with you is a bat
and ball. How do you get out?
You try to hit the ball once.
You miss. Striiiiike 1.
You try to hit the ball again.
You miss. Striiiiike 2.
You try to hit the ball again.
You miss. Striiiiiiike 3.
You're outta there!

What's the world's fastest sport?
Quicket.

When do tennis players go to bed?
Tennish.

How do football players stay
cool under pressure?
They stand next to the fans.

Arnold Schwarzenegger once owned a sports shop. One day, a customer asked if he had any baseball bats. Arnold replied, **"Aisle B, back."**

I told a friend I had a job in a bowling alley. "Tenpin?" they asked. "No," I said, "it's permanent."

Two friends lived together – one worked in the city and the other worked from home making tennis equipment for giants. On a particularly busy day, the tennis-equipment maker was up until 2 a.m., and his housemate couldn't sleep through the noise. Finally, the housemate couldn't take it anymore, so stormed out of her bedroom and shouted, "Look, I'm trying to sleep. Can you stop making such a big racket?"

What type of race is never run?
A swimming race.

Why did the ballerina give up?
It was tutu hard.

What is the hardest part of skydiving?
The ground.

I kept wondering why the football
was getting bigger and bigger.
Then it hit me.

How did the physicist work out?
By pumping ion.

**What did the football team do
when their pitch got flooded?
Brought on the subs!**

It was another ordinary day at the local swimming pool.

Lifeguard: Sir, I'm sorry, but you are officially banned from the swimming pool.

Swimmer: Why? Have I done something wrong?

Lifeguard: I saw you take a pee in the swimming pool!

Swimmer: That's not fair! Surely I'm not the only one who does that?

Lifeguard: You're the only one who climbs up and does it from the top of the diving board.

Why are Canadians so awesome at sports?
They always bring their eh game!

**What do you call a girl in the
middle of a tennis court?
Annette.**

I used to have a fear of hurdles,
but I got over it.

How do you start a firefly race?
Ready, set, glow!

Why can't you tell jokes while ice skating?
In case the ice cracks up.

The local tennis club's website is down.
**They're having problems
with their server.**

What did the baseball glove say to the ball?
Catch you later!

Why did the chicken get sent off?
Persistent fowl play!

What does the sun use to skate on?
Solarblades!

Why was the basketball court flooded?
The players dribbled all over it.

Where do American
footballers go when they need
a replacement uniform?
New Jersey.

What does a cyclist
ride in winter?
An icicle.

What position does a ghost
play in football?
Ghoulie!

**What animal is best at
hitting a baseball?
A bat.**

What kind of cats go bowling?
Alley cats.

**I'm completely sick of martial arts.
I think I have kung flu.**

CHAPTER SEVEN

SCHOOL SILLINESS

They are the best – and worst – days of our lives. For every soggy school dinner and tricky science test, there's kiss chase and the end-of-day bell! So, even though school's *out* for some, it's definitely *in* this joke book.

Why was six afraid of seven?
Because seven, eight, nine.

**What happens when the number of
bullies at a school goes up?
The mean increases.**

What's white when it's dirty
and black when it's clean?
A blackboard.

**Did you hear about the teacher who tied
all the class's shoelaces together?
They went on a class trip!**

A girl came in from her first day at school and her mother asked, "What did you learn today?" "Not enough," replied the girl, "they said I have to go back tomorrow."

Teacher: What is the chemical formula for water?
Student: H-I-J-K-L-M-N-O.
Teacher: What are you talking about?
Student: Last week you said it was H to O.

Why didn't the human anatomy
professor tell her students they
dissected the wrong body?
She didn't have the heart to.

**When I was at school someone
stole my mood ring.
I'm still not sure how I feel about it.**

I made it through school maths while
only remembering even numbers.
What are the odds?

A student asked their teacher if
they could be excused as they were
desperate to go to the toilet.
The teacher said, "Only if you can say
the entire alphabet before you go."
The student quickly said,
"abcdefghijklmnoqrstuvwxyz."
The teacher said, "Hey! Where's the p?"
The student said, "Halfway down my leg."

I had my school reunion last weekend. I ran into the Smith twins and thought, well, they both still look exactly the same.

At school some kids offered me money to hang out with them.
It was clique bait.

Why did the girl wear glasses
in her maths class?
It improves de-vision.

**Ever since I took geometry at school, I feel
like my life has turned around 360 degrees.**

Why are history teachers so
good at finding partners?
They love dates.

**My kid asked if I'd pay some of their
limousine cost for the school prom.
It was a bit of a stretch.**

A teacher arrived in class to see a student frantically eating page after page after page of their homework. The teacher was stunned and asked, "Why on earth are you eating your homework?" The student looked up and said, "Because I don't have a dog."

Did you hear about the
kidnapping at school?
**It's OK, they woke up before
the teacher noticed.**

**What do you do if a teacher
rolls their eyes at you?
Pick them up and roll them back.**

Knock, knock.
Who's there?
Dewey.
Dewey who?
Dewey have to go to school today?

Who invented King Arthur's round table?
Sir Cumference.

**A teacher asked their class how
many seconds are in a year.
A student put her hand up.
The teacher, impressed, said, "Yes?"
The student replied, "It's twelve."
The teacher said, "How's that?"
"January second, February second,
March second…"**

A school pupil decided to become a bank robber rather than finish high school. On their first hold-up they pulled out a gun, pointed it at a bank clerk and said, "Give me all the money or you're geography!" The confused clerk was about to put the money in the bag but stopped to ask, "Did you mean to say, 'history'?" The robber said, "Stop changing the subject!"

Teacher: Why is your homework
in your father's handwriting?
Pupil: Because I used his pen.

**One day at school I lost my thesaurus.
I couldn't find the words to
tell you how upset I was.**

Why did the music teacher need a ladder?
To reach the high notes.

What's a teacher's favourite nation?
Expla-nation!

**What was the wizard's
favourite class at school?
Spelling.**

What did one maths book say
to the other maths book?
I've got problems to solve.

**Why did the teacher wear sunglasses?
His students were so bright.**

One day, a teacher decided that she would treat her class. She said, "Whichever pupil answers my next question can go home early today." Just then, when the teacher had her back turned, a pupil grabbed an eraser and threw it at the board. The teacher asked angrily, "Who just threw that?" The pupil said, "I did! I'm going home now."

A teacher asked their student,
"Are you ignorant or just apathetic?"
**To which the student replied,
"I don't know and I don't care!"**

**Why did the cross-eyed
teacher lose their job?
They couldn't control their pupils.**

Why didn't four ask two to the prom?
He was two squared.

What did the buffalo say to his child
when he dropped him off at school?
Bison.

**What's the difference between
a teacher and a train?**
**The teacher will tell you to spit out the
gum but a train will say "chew, chew!"**

Early one morning, a mother
went in to wake up her son.
"Wake up! It's time to go to school."
"But I don't want to go."
"Give me two reasons why
you don't want to go."
"Well, for one, the kids hate me, and
two, the teachers hate me as well!"
"Oh, come on, that's no reason not
to go. Get up and get ready."
"Give me two reasons why
I should go to school."
"Well, for one, you're 56 years old. And
for another, you're the headmaster!"

Why don't farts graduate from school?
They always get expelled.

What did one calculator say to the other?
You can count on me.

I didn't see you at camouflage school today.
Good work.

**My favourite teacher at school
was a lady called Miss Turtle.
She tortoise well.**

When I left school I passed every single exam except Greek Mythology.
It was my Achilles kneecap.

What vegetables do librarians like?
Quiet peas.

The English teacher had decided
that today she would teach spelling.
She turned to the class and asked
one of her pupils, "How do you
spell 'wrong'?" The student said,
"R-O-N-G." The teacher said, "No,
that's wrong." So the student said,
"That's what you asked for!"

Why is a maths book always unhappy?
Because it has a lot of problems.

What school do giraffes go to?
High school.

What do you call a square
that's had an accident?
A wrecktangle.

What flies around school at night?
The alphabat.

Who is the king of stationery?
The ruler.

Why doesn't the sun go to school?
It already has a million degrees.

Why did the school ban scissors?
So people wouldn't cut class.

Why did the student drown?
Their grades were below C–level.

Why did the echo get detention?
For answering back.

How do sea creatures get to school?
Octobus.

Teacher: Name two pronouns.
Pupil: Who, me?
Teacher: Very good!

**Who was the first person
to invent fractions?
Henry the eighth.**

What do elves learn in school?
The elfabet.

What is a polygon?
A dead parrot.

How do you get straight As at school?
Use a ruler.

I just saw my maths teacher lock himself
in his office with a piece of graph paper.
He must be plotting something.

CHAPTER EIGHT

MONSTER MERRIMENT

Monsters: they're creepy and they're kooky, mysterious and spooky. It's time for the bogeyman hiding in your closet, the ghouls who haunt your cellar and the eight-legged freaks who send shivers down your spine to get us all screaming with laughter.

What sort of ghost hates millennials?
A boo-mer.

**What did the maths teacher
say to the vampire?
Count, Dracula.**

How does a monster start a fairy tale?
"Once upon a slime..."

**What's the one thing zombies really want?
Piece of mind.**

Last Halloween I got a job in a factory
making chocolate Draculas.
**There were only two of us, so I had
to make every second count.**

**I took out a loan to pay for an exorcism.
If I don't pay it back, I'm going
to get repossessed!**

What did the ghost say when
it had a hangover?
I need to lay off the boos.

**I'm thinking of opening a hotel for zombies.
A dead and breakfast.**

What do you call a vampire
that never leaves?
A pain in the neck.

An explorer had captured King Kong. He reached toward the captive animal, but as soon as he touched the gorilla's fur, King Kong went berserk and burst from the cage. The explorer ran for his life through jungles and rivers all the way to the coast. He realized the only option was to dive into the sea and hope King Kong couldn't swim. To his horror, the gorilla jumped in and demonstrated a superb front crawl. On they swam across the Atlantic until four months later they reached Brazil. The man collapsed as King Kong prodded him with a giant paw and said, "You're it!"

Two monsters were eating a clown.
One turned to the other and said,
"Does this guy taste a bit funny?"

**A skeleton walked into a café and said,
"I'll have a coffee and a mop..."**

What's the first thing a monster eats
after it's been to the dentist?
The dentist.

What do ghosts eat for dessert?
Ice scream!

What did Frankenstein say when
his monster spat at him?
It's saliva!

What do you call a witch with a rash?
An itchy witchy.

A man, his wife and a friend were running from zombies during the apocalypse. They finally found shelter when the man noticed blood on his wife's shirt. "Darling, what's that on your clothes?" he asked. "Nothing!" she said, turning away. The man pulled her shirt to reveal a nasty bite mark. The friend noticed and said, "You have to kill her, for our safety." "But I love her, I won't do it!" he replied. The friend said, "Fine, but we both know it's going to come back to bite you."

What has a green spotty body, twelve hairy legs and big eyes on stalks?
I don't know, but there is one crawling up your leg!

How did the monster cure his sore throat?
He spent a lot of time gargoyling.

Who did Frankenstein take to the dance?
His ghoulfriend.

My dad asked me why there was a
lion and a witch in my wardrobe.
I said it's Narnia business.

What does Jaws put on his toast?
Buuuuuh-tah. Buuuuuh-tah.
Buh-tah, buh-tah, buh-tah...

One day a man called Adam
came across a witch.
Witch: "Tell me I'm pretty,
or I'll curse you!"
Adam: "Sorry, but I don't
find you attractive."
So the witch cast a spell and
transformed him into an ant.
Witch: "Look at what your
rudeness has cost you!"
Adam: "Yeah, this sucks, but
you still look rotten!"
Witch: "Very well. You will remain
like this until you call me pretty!"
He's still adamant.

Two ghosts walked into a bar.
**The bartender said, "Sorry,
we don't serve spirits."**

**What did the skeleton order
at the restaurant?
Spare ribs.**

Why are vampires easy to fool?
Because they're suckers.

What do you call a vampire
with a really bad cold?
Nosfer-achoo!

**A big, scary gorilla came to my
house and rang the bell.
King Kong!**

What do you call two spiders
that have just got married?
Newlywebbed.

**What do you call a ghost who built
his business from nothing?
A hauntrepreneur.**

Three vampires walked into a bar and sat down. The bartender went over to take their orders. "What can I get you gentlemen?" The first vampire said, "I'll have a glass of blood." The second vampire said, "I'll have a glass of blood, too." The third vampire said, "I'll go for something different and have a glass of plasma." The bartender said, "Right, so two bloods and a blood light."

Me and a friend dressed as
Peruvian owls for Halloween.
We were Inca Hoots.

**Why do mummies have so much
trouble keeping friends?**
They're too wrapped up in themselves.

Why don't vampires have many friends?
Because they're a pain in the neck!

How do you annoy Dracula?

Make him a little cross.

Why don't mummies go on holiday?

They don't want to unwind too much.

There once was a very, very stubborn witch. She would never, ever accept help from her friends. She would always insist on fighting her enemies alone, saying she didn't want to rely on anyone else. One time, she came up against a really tough enemy and ended up losing the fight and became trapped forever in a crystal necklace. Now she's really in-de-pendent.

What do sea monsters have for dinner?
Fish and ships.

How does Dracula like to decorate his house?
Fang shui!

A ghost walked into the bar –
he just wanted some boos.

What do you get if you cross
a vampire and a snowman?
Frost bite.

How do vampires get into houses?
Through the bat flap.

**What do you get when you cross a
cocker spaniel, a poodle and a ghost?
A cocker poodle boo!**

Two sea monsters were relaxing in the ocean. A ship full of potatoes sailed by and the first sea monster gobbled it up immediately. Then, a second ship full of potatoes sailed by and the monster gobbled that up as well! After seeing this happen several more times, the other sea monster turned to the first and said, "Wow, are you hungry or what? What's with you and these ships?" The first sea monster replied, "Oh, you know how it is. Nobody can ever eat just one potato ship!"

What kind of monster sits at
the end of your finger?
The bogeyman.

Why are ghosts bad liars?
You can see right through them.

Why did the vampire go
and see the doctor?
They couldn't stop coffin.

What's a zombie's favourite drink?
A stiff one.

What did the postman deliver to Dracula?
Fang mail.

What kind of monster has the best hearing?
The eeriest.

Why did the skeleton not cross the road?
They didn't have the guts.

I'm starting to think my
girlfriend is really a ghost.
**I had my suspicions the moment
she walked through the door.**

**What is a mummy's
favourite type of music?
Wrap.**

Did you hear about the twin witches?
No one knew witch was witch.

I offered a zombie a bit of my dinner.
He bit my hand off.

**What do you find most between
Godzilla's toes?
Slow runners.**

MONSTER MERRIMENT

Where do baby ghosts go
during the day?
The dayscare centre.

**How did Frankenstein get
around the city?
Monster truck.**

I used to date a ghost,
but he was too possessive.

**Witches don't fart;
they cast smells.**

CHAPTER NINE

NATURE NONSENSE

From colourful bouncing insects to tall trees and gorgeous sunrises, nature never fails to astonish us with its ravishing beauty. But it's not all about picturesque views – Mother Nature has a sense of humour, too!

One day there was a knock on a woman's door. She answered but couldn't see anyone. She was about to shut the door when she looked down and saw a tiny little snail. The woman looked confused so leaned down, picked up the snail and threw it as far as the eye could see. Twenty years later the woman heard a knock again. She answered it and miraculously saw the exact same snail. The snail looked up and said, "Why did you do that?"

Did you know the colour blue
doesn't exist in nature?
It's just a pigment of your imagination.

**What did the hurricane say
to the sports car?
Wanna go for a spin?**

Why did the mushroom go to the party?
Because he was a fun-gi.

Two fish were swimming in a stream when it started raining. **One looked at the other and said, "Quick, let's swim under that bridge before we get wet."**

One time I stayed up all night figuring out where the sun went at the end of the day. Then it dawned on me.

A man in a cinema sat down and noticed that he was sitting next to a grasshopper. Quite puzzled by this spectacle, he turned and said, "Excuse me, are you a grasshopper?" "Yes," replied the grasshopper. "But what are you doing at the cinema?" asked the man. The grasshopper replied, "Well, I liked the book."

What are caterpillars scared of?
Dogerpillars.

I trod on a snail this morning.
It looked crushed.

What looks like half a leaf?
The other half of a leaf.

What's green and has wheels?
Grass. I was joking about the wheels.

Knock, knock.
Who's there?
Snow business.
Snow business who?
Snow business like show business.

I gave the sun a rating.
One star.

A lumberjack was out in the forest
for another day of tree felling.
As he started his chainsaw, he heard
a tree begin to cry. "Please don't
cut me down!" it pleaded, "I'll do
anything!" The lumberjack said,
"OK, if you can solve this impossible
riddle that has fooled some of the
greatest minds since the beginning of
time to the present day, I shall spare
you." But the tree was stumped.

How did the bee greet the flower?
Hey, honey.

**I hate it when spiders eat flies.
Such a buzzkill!**

What did one firefly say to the other?
You GLOW girl!

**Nature is incredibly resourceful.
It can make dew with just water.**

What is the difference between
weather and climate?
**You can't weather a tree,
but you can climate.**

**Doctor, doctor, I keep
thinking I'm a caterpillar.
Don't worry, you'll soon change.**

A dung beetle walked into a bar
and said, "Is this stool taken?"

What do you call a group of church-
going sisters in a flower shop?
Nuns and Roses.

Why can't you trust atoms?
They make up everything.

What do you say when a beach
asks you to walk on it?
Shore.

What crime is punishable by death
in the kingdom of trees?
Tree-son.

A woman was wandering through the desert, lost and absolutely starving, when she saw a bacon tree in the distance. She stumbled through the heat toward it but when she finally arrived a robber stepped out and pointed a gun at her. The hungry woman said, "Please, I'm starving, I've been wandering for days. I just wanted to get some bacon from the bacon tree!" The robber said, "This ain't no bacon tree, this is a hambush!"

Doctor, doctor, I looked at the
sun through a colander.
**Hmm, yes, I can see you've
strained your eyes.**

**I was going to grow some herbs
but couldn't find the thyme.**

My boyfriend was angry when I tried
to plant flowers on his head.
I think they'll grow on him.

I won gold at a weather forecasting
tournament yesterday.
I beat the raining champion.

**Have you heard about that new river film?
It's streaming now.**

What do you call a spider with twenty eyes?
Spiiiiiiiiiiiiiiiiiiiiider.

**What should you wear when you
go walking in a storm?
Wind socks.**

A sun walked casually into a black
hole. The black hole tutted and said,
"Hey, sun, I don't think you appreciate
the gravity of this situation."

What do clouds do when they get rich?
Make it rain!

Tourists in a history museum were marvelling at dinosaur bones. One of them asked the guide "Can you tell me how old these bones are?" The guide replied, "They are 65,000,011 years old." "That's an awfully exact number," said the tourist. "How can you know their age so precisely?" The guide answered, "Well, the dinosaur bones were sixty-five million years old when I started working here, and that was eleven years ago."

Why was the lightning
always getting into trouble?
**It didn't know how to
conduct itself!**

**What did one volcano say to the other?
I lava you.**

Did you hear about the snail
who lost his shell?
He looked sluggish.

Why are mountains so funny?
Because they're hilly areas.

What's the opposite of a hot yes?
A cold snow.

What goes up when
the rain comes down?
An umbrella.

Why are mountains always sleepy?
Because they don't Everest.

The four seasons were arguing
about which of them was the best.
Winter said, "In winter you can
build snowmen and the snow
is so fun. And I have Christmas,
everyone loves Christmas!"
Spring laughed, "Sure, but come
springtime, everything is so fresh
and beautiful! There are new flowers,
and rays of sunny hope. It doesn't
get much better than that!"
Summer said, "Yes, but I am
undoubtedly the best season! Days
at the beach, ice cream, nice weather.
You can't top that. What about you
autumn, what do you offer?"
Autumn: *leaves*

What do snails use to get the
shells on their back so shiny?
Snail varnish.

**Why do you need to watch out
when it's raining cats and dogs?
In case you step in a poodle!**

What did the ocean say to the beach?
Nothing, it just waved.

How does a flower whistle?
With their tulips.

When is the moon at its heaviest?
When it's full.

I'm really worried about my boyfriend and this weather. Ever since it started snowing, he's seemed really down. We've had strong, cold winds blowing lately, and freezing rain forming layers of ice over the snow. All he does is stand at the window, staring, and I think he might be getting a bit down about it. In fact, if this nasty weather keeps up, I might need to let him come back inside.

What do you get when you cross
an insect with a rabbit?
Bugs Bunny.

What's the world's biggest moth?
A mammoth.

Why did the man throw butter
out of the window?
To see butterfly!

**My friend told me I planted
the wrong flowers.
Ooopsie daisy.**

After a long year wiggling around,
what did the caterpillar decide
to do on New Year's Day?
Turn over a new leaf.

**Why do trees act suspiciously
when it's sunny outside?
I don't know, but there's always been
something a little shady about them.**

Frodo and Sam were sitting outside, observing an insect. Neither of them was quite sure what kind of insect it was. "Is it a wasp?" said Frodo, to which Sam replied, "No, Mister Frodo, I think it's some kind of bee." Then they saw Gandalf walking by and asked him whether he knew what kind of insect it was. He looked at the insect for just the briefest of moments before replying, "Fly, you fools!"

How do bees brush their hair?
With a honeycomb.

What did one leaf say to the other?
I'm falling for you.

What type of shorts do clouds wear?
Thunderpants.

How do you chop a wave in half?
Use a sea-saw.

What do you find at the top of a mountain?
Summit.

CHAPTER TEN

RANDOM RIB-TICKLERS!

Not all things that tickle our funny bones can be easily categorized. So, here's to the silly bits and bobs that make us guffaw and blow high-speed snot bubbles from our nostrils.

What's Whitney Houston's
favourite type of coordination?
Hand-eyyyyyyyyyyye.

**Did you hear about the clairvoyant
who got robbed?
He never saw it coming.**

A clown turned up for work late on his first
day and he got sacked from the circus.
He's suing for funfair dismissal.

**Last week I stole a calendar.
I got twelve months.**

I went into a DVD shop and said to the man behind the counter, "Can I have *Batman Forever?*" he said, "No, you have to bring it back tomorrow."

I went to a vinyl shop to buy a new record. I said, "Have you got anything by The Doors?" The assistant said, "An umbrella and a bucket with some sand."

Doctor, doctor, I need your help. Have you got anything for excessive wind? **Here, have this kite.**

Doctor, doctor, my stomach keeps making strange sounds like "Aaa", "Eeee", "I", "Ohhh" and "You". **I think you might have irritable vowel syndrome.**

A man walked into a restaurant and ordered some bread, then asked, "Oh, is that gluten-free?" The waiter replied, "No, but it's very reasonably priced."

Arnold Schwarzenegger was sitting in his office on Easter Sunday with a big sulky face. Everybody seemed to have forgotten to send him any Easter eggs! He started to cry a little bit. Upon hearing the commotion his assistant popped their head round the door and said, "Aww Arnold, are you OK?" He immediately brightened up, cracked a big, toothy smile and said, "It's OK, I still love Easter, baby!"

I was in a Chinese restaurant the other day when this duck walked up to me with a red rose and said, "Your eyes are like the blue of the deepest ocean." I said, "Waiter, I asked for A-ROMATIC duck."

Doctor, doctor, when I stand up quickly I see Donald Duck and Mickey Mouse.
Hmm, how long have you been having these Disney spells?

Did you hear about the wig who
got kicked out of the bar?
It was off its head.

**I slept like a log last night.
I woke up in the fireplace.**

Sometimes I tuck my knees tight
against my chest and lean forward.
That's how I roll.

**What's the difference between a
good joke and a bad joke timing.**

An Englishman, a Frenchman, a Spaniard and a German were all enjoying a wonderful day together. They'd gathered to watch a street performer who was doing some juggling. The juggler noticed that the group didn't seem to have a very good view, so decided to stand on a wooden box to help them see him better. He shouted, "Can everyone see me now?"

They replied in turn...

"Yes!"

"Oui!"

"Sí!"

"Ja!"

Did you hear about the pirates who
had eyepatches on opposite eyes?
They never did see eye to eye.

**What did the pirate say when
his false leg got wet?
Shiver me timbers.**

What did the pirate say
when he turned 80?
Arrr–matey.

I asked the colonel what the lowest rank
in the army was. He said, "It's Private."
I said, "Come on, you can tell me."

**Have you seen Captain Corelli's Mandolin?
Yes!
Oh great, can you tell him? He's
been looking for it everywhere.**

Two bits of road were sitting in a bar, boasting about how tough they were. The first one said, "I'm hard as nails because I'm a three-lane highway and have a million cars go over me every year." "Oh yeah?" said the road next to him. "Well, I'm a bridge and have a million trains and two million cars go over me each year." Just then, the door swung open and another bit of road strolled in. The two roads ducked behind their bar stools until he'd gone. The bartender said, "If you're so tough, why are you so scared of him?" The roads replied, "You want to watch out for him, he's a cycle path."

I just had an interview for a job and the interviewer asked me, "Can you perform under pressure?" "No," I said, "But I do a brilliant Bohemian Rhapsody."

Did you hear about the child who just knew he was going to be a pop star? He was Adam Ant.

A man walked into an airport and said, "Cluck cluck, bacawww!" **The attendant replied, "I'm sorry, this is the check-in desk."**

Doctor, doctor, I can't stop stealing things.
Take these pills, and if they don't work, I'll have a sports car.

Doctor, doctor, I think I'm addicted to brake fluid.
That's rubbish, you can stop anytime.

Doctor, doctor, I think I've swallowed a dictionary.
Less words, more rest for you.

Doctor, doctor, I think I've broken my arm in two places.
You should stop going to those places.

A pirate walked into a doctor's clinic. "Strike me down, yarrr," they growled, clearly in some pain. "I wants ye to look at the moles on me back. I think they're multiplyin'." The doctor thought it serious enough for inspection and took a look at the pirate's back. "It's OK," the doctor said with a smile, "they're benign." "Arrr, are ye sure?" asked the pirate, "I'm pretty sure there be ten."

I've just started reading a
horror story in Braille.
**Something terrible is going
to happen; I can feel it.**

**I backed a horse the other day at ten
to one; it came in at quarter past six!**

As a scarecrow, people say I'm outstanding
in my field. But hay, it's in my jeans.

I rang up my mobile phone company the other day and said, "I want to report a nuisance caller." They replied, "Not you again."

I was mugged by six dwarves last night. Not Happy.

A man walked into a bar and ordered a beer. Then he pulled out hundreds of pink Valentine's Day cards, wrote inside them and stamped them with "Love" stamps. He then pulled out a bottle of expensive perfume and spritzed each envelope. The bartender couldn't contain their curiosity and said, "You must have 500 cards there! I've got to admit I'm curious what you're doing." The man replied, "Every year on Valentine's Day I send out 500 cards, each one signed 'Guess Who'." "But, why?" the bartender asked. "I'm a divorce lawyer," the man replied.

Why are pirates called pirates?
Because they arrrrrrrr!

**How much did the pirate pay for
their piercings?
A buck-an-ear.**

Why is being a pirate so addictive?
**Because once you lose a hand,
you're hooked.**

**How do you make a pirate furious?
Take away the "p".**

I was going to go to the doctor's because I had a blemish all over my neck, but I ended up going to the beach instead.
That was a rash decision.

I said to the travel agent, "I want to go to Paris, please." They said, "Eurostar?" I said, "I've been on TV, but I'm no Oprah."

A group of chess enthusiasts checked in to a hotel and were standing in the lobby discussing their recent tournament victories. One said, "I've won many, many international tournaments." Another said, "I'm unbeaten for two years." Until one more said, "Well, I've been world champion ten times!" After about an hour of this chess boasting, the manager came out of the office and asked them to go on their way. "But why?" they asked the manager. "Because I can't stand chess nuts boasting in an open foyer."

What's the best thing about Switzerland?
Well, the flag is a big plus.

**How do you find Will Smith
when it's snowing?
You look for the fresh prints.**

Waiter, waiter! What's this
fly doing in my soup?
Looks like backstroke to me.

Russian dolls? Absolutely full of themselves.

What dinosaur has the best vocabulary?
The thesaurus.

Did you hear about the pirate
who loved yoga?
He kept doing the plank.

I once paid twenty pounds to watch
Prince but partied like it was £19.99.

Why is Blondie bad with directions?
**She says you have to go
"One way, or another."**

**What did the right eye say to the left eye?
Something smells between us.**

What did they give the guy who
invented the door knocker?
The no-bell prize.

What do you call a wizard who walks everywhere on bare feet, has poor bone density and really bad breath?
A super-calloused fragile mystic hexed by halitosis.

I just found out that my friend has a secret life as a priest.
It's his altar ego.

Have you tried that new coconut shampoo?
It leaves your coconuts looking fabulous.

And the award for best neckwear goes to...
... well, would you look at that, it's a tie!

What do you call a Frenchman
wearing sandals?
Philippe Falop.

How do you keep an idiot in suspense?

If you're interested in finding out more about our books, find us on Facebook at **Summersdale Publishers** and follow us on Twitter at **@Summersdale**.

www.summersdale.com